Measuring Performance

Pocket Mentor Series

The *Pocket Mentor* Series offers immediate solutions to common challenges managers face on the job every day. Each book in the series is packed with handy tools, self-tests, and real-life examples to help you identify your strengths and weaknesses and hone critical skills. Whether you're at your desk, in a meeting, or on the road, these portable guides enable you to tackle the daily demands of your work with greater speed, savvy, and effectiveness.

Books in the series

Becoming a New Manager
Coaching People
Creating a Business Plan
Delegating Work
Developing Employees
Dismissing an Employee
Executing Innovation
Executing Strategy
Giving Feedback
Giving Presentations
Hiring an Employee
Laying Off Employees

Leading People
Leading Teams
Making Decisions
Managing Change
Managing Crises
Managing Difficult Interactions
Managing Diversity
Managing Projects
Managing Stress
Managing Time
Managing Up

Measuring Performance

Expert Solutions to Everyday Challenges

Harvard Business Press

Boston, Massachusetts

Library of Congress Cataloging information available.

ISBN 978-1-4221-2970-8

The paper used in this publication meets the requirements of the American National
Standard for Permanence of Paper for Publications and Documents in Libraries
and Archives Z39.48-1992.

Contents

Measuring Performance: The Basics

Tips and Tools

Test Yourself   87

A helpful review of concepts presented in this guide. Take it before and after you've read the guide, to see how much you've learned.

Answers to test questions   90

To Learn More   95

Further titles of articles and books if you want to go more deeply into the topic.

Sources for Measuring Performance   101

Key Terms   103

Notes   109

For you to use as ideas come to mind.

Mentor's Message: Why Measure Organizational Performance?

In an age of intensifying competition and rapid change, organizations must constantly seek to enhance their performance: their ability to generate important business results such as increased shareholder value, greater customer loyalty, more responsive and efficient business processes, and better productivity and alignment of their employees to strategic objectives. But you can't manage what you don't measure. How can executives determine whether the company is creating the conditions for greater shareholder value unless they track changes in their critical performance metrics over time?

As a manager, you play a vital role in measuring performance in your organization. For example, you might assess your unit's contributions to the company's profitability, productivity, customer loyalty, innovation, and other key performance indicators defined by executives. You will want to learn how to select and track performance measures for your unit. This book explains how performance measurement works, how to take a systematic approach to it, and how to avoid common mistakes.

Robert S. Kaplan, Mentor

Robert S. Kaplan is Baker Foundation Professor at the Harvard Business School and Chairman of the Practice Leadership Committee of Palladium, Executing Strategy. Kaplan's research, teaching, and consulting focus on linking cost and performance management systems to strategy implementation and operational excellence. He has been a codeveloper of both activity-based costing and the Balanced Scorecard. He has authored or coauthored fourteen books, eighteen *Harvard Business Review* articles, and more than one hundred twenty other papers.

His books on performance measurement, coauthored with David Norton, include *The Execution Premium*; *Alignment*; *Strategy Maps: Converting Intangible Assets into Tangible Outcomes* (named as one of the top ten business books of 2004 by *Strategy & Business* and amazon.com); *The Strategy-Focused Organization: How Balanced Scorecard Companies Thrive in the New Business Environment* (named by Cap Gemini Ernst & Young as the best international business book for year 2000); and *The Balanced Scorecard: Translating Strategy into Action*, which has been translated into twenty-two languages and has won the 2001 Wildman Medal from the American Accounting Association for its impact on the practice of accounting.

Measuring Performance: The Basics

An Overview of Performance Measurement

Do you jog, play basketball, ride a bike, or participate in some other team or individual sport? If so, you likely keep track of your performance, even if it's as simple as "I ran that eight-mile loop faster than ever" or "I scored four more points during this game than I did in the last one."

Why do you keep score in these ways? Like many people, you're probably performance-driven or achievement-oriented—or maybe just naturally competitive. You want to know whether your performance is improving or declining and how your latest achievement compares with your personal best. You crave feedback on how you're doing.

In much the same way, organizations want—and need—to track the changes in their overall performance. And the divisions, units, teams, and individuals within them engage in similar score-keeping.

Let's take a closer look at this desire to measure business performance.

Why appraise business performance?

Organizations measure their performance for numerous reasons. Here are just a few:

- **Improvement:** By tracking performance, companies can spot—and promptly address—problems such as declining customer loyalty, flattening profits, or defections of talented employees.

- **Planning and forecasting:** Performance measurement serves as a progress check, enabling organizations to determine whether they're meeting their goals and whether they need to revise their budgets and forecasts.

- **Competition:** When companies compare their perform-ance against their rivals' and against industry benchmarks, they can identify weak areas and address them to sharpen their competitive edge.

- **Reward:** By knowing how much employees have excelled in achieving goals, managers can distribute performance-based incentives and rewards fairly to their direct reports.

- **Regulatory and standards compliance:** Many companies measure performance in order to comply with government regulations (such as antipollution laws) or international standards (for instance, ISO 9000).

You can't manage what you can't measure.
—Peter Drucker

What is performance measurement?

In its simplest terms, measuring performance means assessing business results to: (1) determine the effectiveness of a company's strategy and the efficiency of its operating processes, and (2) make changes to address shortfalls and other problems.

Companies take stock of their performance using different methods and criteria. However, in many organizations, performance measurement entails examining the results generated by key business activities, using specific *performance metrics* (also known as measures). For each business activity, there are numerous possible metrics. Table 1 shows just a few examples.

Many organizations use a coordinated system, or framework, to appraise business performance across their functions. The best performance measurement systems demonstrate balance:

- They assess a company's financial performance (such as revenues, expenses, and profits) *and* nonfinancial performance (for example, employee knowledge, information systems availability, and quality of customer relationships).

- They draw on internal data (such as process quality) *and* external data (for example, third-party rankings of companies' product performance against competitors').

- They examine lagging (backward-looking) indicators *and* leading (forward-looking) indicators. For instance, sales figures show you what your company has achieved in the past and thus are a lagging indicator. By contrast, customer-satisfaction ratings suggest how your customers may behave in the future; thus they constitute a leading indicator.

- They weigh subjective (difficult to quantify) aspects of performance (such as customer satisfaction and employee capabilities) *and* objective (easy to quantify) aspects (for example, revenues and return on invested capital).

TABLE 1

Specific performance metrics

Business activity	Possible performance metrics
Finance	• Profit margin (percentage of every dollar of sales that contributes to the company's bottom line) • Revenues • Return on invested capital
Marketing	• Market share • Customer loyalty • Customer profitability
Production	• Number of units manufactured within a specific time period • Number of items shipped on time • Machine change-over time
Sales	• Percentage of customer visits or phone calls that generate sales • Percentage increase in sales over previous quarter or year • Percentage of customers retained this period
Customer service	• Number of customer complaints • Service-call response time
Purchasing	• Vendors' ability to provide services or materials on time • Defect rate of vendors' products
Quality	• Product yield: ratio of good products produced to total products started into production • Defect rates of a key process
Human resources	• Workforce turnover • Employee skills • Employee motivation

By striking a balance in its performance measurement system, a company compiles a more complete picture of how it's doing. This comprehensive picture enables executives and managers to learn from mistakes, constantly improve, and make the smartest possible decisions.

Indeed, some managers draw an analogy between effective performance measurement and the operation of an airplane: to fly a plane, a pilot must look at many instruments—airspeed indicator, fuel gauge, altitude indicator, GPS map, and so forth—rather than rely on a single instrument that provides just one piece of information. Similarly, organizations seeking to navigate through a complex environment need a range of "instruments" to evaluate how they're doing. Effective performance measurement provides that comprehensive range of information with which a company can gauge its performance.

Who uses performance measurement data?

Many people inside and outside a company use performance measurement data. For instance, *executives* use the data to review how well corporate strategy is being implemented and whether major corrective actions need to be taken. *Unit managers* and *group leaders* use performance data to motivate and evaluate employee performance and productivity. *Shareholders, industry analysts, customers, media*, and *government regulators* use data to make choices such as whether to invest in or buy from a company, or to determine whether an organization is operating with efficiency and integrity. And *employees* learn whether they and their teams are contributing to company goals.

Does your boss require you to track specific aspects of your group's performance? If not, should you still take time to learn about performance measurement and assess your group's business results? The answer is yes! Why? Assessing your group's results—and understanding the value of performance measurement in general—enables you to:

- Determine whether you and your direct reports are helping your company to achieve its goals.

- Correct any missteps or flaws in order to improve your group's performance.

- Understand how your behavior and choices affect your employees' performance.

- Identify new opportunities for your unit or group to improve its effectiveness or even extend its contribution to the company's success.

- Build your business knowledge and professional credibility—and thereby further your career.

Understanding Key Performance Indicators

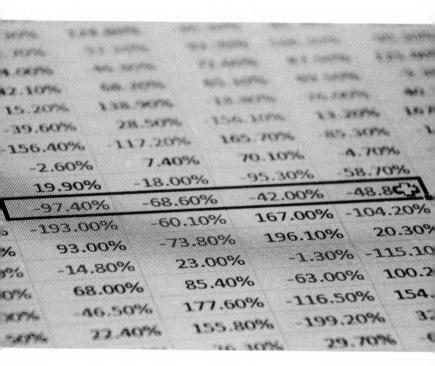

Some companies have formal, enterprisewide performance measurement systems in place (such as Six Sigma, the Plan-Do-Check-Act methodology, or the Balanced Scorecard). Such systems enable executives to look across the organization's business activities to gain a holistic view of the company's performance. Other companies use a simpler approach, appraising the performance of one or more discrete aspects of the business.

Regardless of the system a company uses, all organizations use key performance indicators to assess their performance.

If you're not keeping score, you're only practicing, not playing.
—Vince Lombardi

What is a KPI?

A *key performance indicator* (KPI) is a measure reflecting how an organization is doing in a specific aspect of its performance. A KPI is one representation of a *critical success factor* (CSF)—a key activity needed to achieve a given strategic objective. Organizations that measure performance identify the handful of critical success factors that comprise every strategic objective.

For example, depending on a company's strategy, the organization might have a KPI for the percentage of income the organization derives from international markets. Another KPI might be the number of customer complaints about orders filled incorrectly. Some organizations use many KPIs for all their different areas of operation. Other enterprises' KPIs may focus on a specific area. For instance, a social service nonprofit may focus all its KPIs on the amount of aid that is granted to different entities.

Typically, each unit within a company also has a set of KPIs that supports the company's goals. Performance data for a unit's KPIs can be rolled up into the company's KPIs to reflect total organizational performance in any given area being measured.

As a manager, you probably won't participate in developing KPIs at the corporate level. However, you may be involved in creating KPIs at your unit's level, especially if your unit was recently acquired or has been associated with a new product, process, department, or line of reporting. Regardless of your situation, you should be aware of the KPIs that are in place in your organization. With this awareness, you can appraise your group's progress toward corporate and unit goals.

Three types of KPIs

Key performance indicators come in three types: First, *process KPIs* measure the efficiency or productivity of a business process. Examples include "Product-repair cycle time," "Days to deliver an order," "Number of rings before a customer phone call is answered," "Number of employees graduating from training programs," and "Weeks required to fill vacant positions."

Second, *input KPIs* measure assets and resources invested in or used to generate business results. Examples include "Dollars spent on research and development," "Funding for employee

What Would YOU Do?

Getting the Big Picture

D ARLENE IS THRILLED about her recent promotion to manager of a product group at TopCo's London division. But a week into the new job, her boss, Tina, calls a meeting with all the group leaders from the division. At the meeting, she explains that she wants to make some changes in how the division is assessing its business performance. "We've been focusing too much on the numbers," she says. "I need a more comprehensive picture of the value our division is generating."

Tina challenges the group leaders to reexamine how they're currently assessing their groups' performance and to propose ideas for change. Darlene leaves the meeting unsure of where to begin.

What would YOU do? The mentor will suggest a solution in *What You COULD Do.*

---

training," "New hires' knowledge and skills," and "Quality of raw materials."

Third, *output KPIs* measure the financial and nonfinancial results of business activities. Examples include "Revenues," "Number of new customers acquired," and "Percentage increase in full-time employees." Three particularly common output KPIs that managers use include:

- **Return on investment (ROI):** Return on investment represents the benefits generated from the use of assets in a company, unit, or group—or on a project. ROI is helpful to top executives, finance managers, board members, and shareholders. A possible way to express return on investment is to divide net income (revenues less expenses less any liabilities, such as taxes) by total assets. ROI measures how effectively managers have used resources and can be figured as follows:

$$ROI = Net\ Income/Total\ Assets$$

- **Economic value added (EVA):** EVA, popularized in the 1990s by U.S. management consultancy Stern Stewart & Co., is defined as the value of a business activity that is left over after you subtract from it the cost of executing that activity and the cost of the physical and financial capital deployed to generate the profits. In the field of corporate finance, EVA is a way to determine the value created, above the required return, for a company's shareholders. It's therefore useful to senior management, boards, and shareholders and other investors. EVA is calculated as follows:

$$EVA = Net\ operating\ profit\ after\ taxes - (net\ operating\ assets \times weighted\ average\ cost\ of\ capital)$$

Shareholders of a company receive a positive EVA when the return from the equity employed in the business's operations is greater than the (risk-adjusted) cost of that capital.

- **Market share:** The percentage of sales in a given industry segment or subsegment captured by your company.

All three types of KPIs—process, input, and output—generate valuable performance information. A mix of the three types ensures a comprehensive picture of your unit's or organization's performance.

KPIs and you

Even if your boss doesn't require you to track process, input, or output KPIs, it's vital that you familiarize yourself with these indicators. Why? For one thing, you may hear these terms used frequently in your organization. Also, you want to understand how your organization defines the determinants of success—for example, where your organization's resource allocation emphasis is. Moreover, in many industries, third-party researchers (such as J.D. Power & Associates) use KPIs to track how your company measures up against the competition. If you consult such research, you'll need to understand KPIs. In addition, these indicators can help you figure out your role in helping your organization achieve its goals. And finally, you'll enhance your credibility and value as a manager if you can demonstrate understanding of your company's and unit's KPIs.

Who uses KPIs?

Managers at all levels in an organization can track key performance indicators to assess how well their groups are meeting their business objectives, whether performance is improving or declining, and how their group's performance compares with that of other units or groups within the company and in rival organizations. Consider these examples:

- A *CEO* examines return on investment by division, or her company's cash flow, by month and quarter, and compares the results with those of competitors.

- A *customer service manager* tracks customer service quality using surveys. If the surveys suggest that service quality is dropping, he might need to add more account representatives to improve service levels.

- A *benefits administrator* monitors how many claims her group has processed during the current year and compares it with the number processed in the previous year. An increase, for example, may suggest it's time to invest in new benefits software that can speed up claims processing.

- A *product development manager* assesses the ratio of sales from new products to total sales. He decides that his group needs to invest more in research and development to increase the ratio.

- A *human resources staffer* calculates the percentage of employees who actually attend voluntary training programs offered by the company and compares the result against the targeted percentage. A drop may indicate the program is unsuccessful and can prompt an inquiry to find out why— possibly saving the company thousands of dollars in ineffective training programs.

What You COULD Do

Remember Darlene's concern about how to measure her group's performance?

Here's what the mentor suggests:

Darlene should first ask Tina to clarify TopCo's and the division's strategies. Darlene realizes that the different ways they gauge success at TopCo work together like a dashboard, showing the state of the company. Based on her understanding of her division's strategy, she and her group will then identify appropriate objectives (or goals) for the group. Next, they'll work together to identify the two or three critical activities they must carry out to achieve those objectives. And they'll translate those actions into a set of performance metrics that express how they'll measure progress on the critical activities. Their metrics will need to reflect a mix of business results—such as sales, customer satisfaction, product innovation, best-practice sharing, staff morale, and operational efficiency. Once Darlene's group has created metrics, they will set targets representing the division's desired performance on each metric and begin gathering data to see how their actual performance compares with the targets they've set. They'll then analyze any gaps between actual and target performance and decide how to respond.

- A *communications expert* reviews employee survey results to see whether workers understand the company's corporate strategy. Lack of understanding may suggest that the company's CEO and other executives need to make clearer presentations on strategy or need to reach employees through different channels.

If you've recently started in your role as manager, you may not yet know which KPIs are used in your unit or group. How might you find out? Ask your boss what measures your group has been using to track performance. If your unit has a business analyst, see if he or she would be available to discuss your unit's KPIs and other performance metrics.

Understanding Performance Measurement Systems

Earlier, we mentioned that many companies use formal performance measurement systems. In this section, we shed additional light on such systems.

What is a formal performance measurement system?

A formal *performance measurement (PM) system* is a set of strategic objectives and performance metrics (including KPIs) applied throughout the entire enterprise. PM systems enable executives to see how business results generated in the company's many different units combine to influence the enterprise's overall results.

Thus, a PM system gives executives and managers a comprehensive, high-level view of their organization's performance and an understanding of how the company's different parts work together to produce business results.

In many companies that use a PM system, senior executives advocate adoption of the system and manage its implementation. But once the system has been established, all managers and employees in the organization contribute to and use it. But how? They define individual goals that support unit- and company-level goals, and they generate performance data that their supervisors then input into the system.

Why are performance measurement systems beneficial?

Performance measurement systems offer numerous benefits. Most important, they enable managers to define (and track performance on) metrics for every strategic objective set by their unit and company. By noting performance that falls short of targets (for example, "Our goal was to reduce order-processing errors 10 percent, but we only reduced them 5 percent"), managers can address the causes of the shortfall and work to continually improve performance.

They also show how performance in different parts of the company affects performance in other parts. For example, a company may discover that having the logistics staff achieve the objective, "Accelerate order-delivery time by 10 percent," helps the customer service group meet its objective, "Increase customer satisfaction by 15 percent." By seeing these interrelationships, companies can make more informed decisions. For instance, they can increase a budget, add new hires, or introduce a more efficient process to improve performance, instead of guessing which factors need to be addressed.

Types of performance measurement systems

There are many different types of performance measurement systems. Next, we examine several of the more commonly used types.

Dashboards or cockpits Possibly the simplest type of PM system, a *dashboard* or *cockpit* combines the company's numerous metrics, targets, and performance data into one online or printed document (such as a spreadsheet) that's prepared monthly, quarterly, or on some other schedule.

Figure 1 shows an example of a dashboard:

FIGURE 1

A dashboard

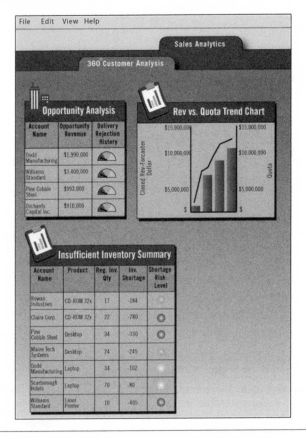

A dashboard enables executives and managers to easily digest the company's aggregated performance data. In addition, many dashboards use a "traffic light" coding system to evaluate performance on each metric, enabling leaders to spot and address problems promptly. For example, red indicates performance that's significantly below target; yellow, slightly below target; green, at or above target.

Although executives have traditionally used dashboards, many companies are now customizing their dashboards for managers at operational levels as well. For instance, at an airline, a manager in charge of stocking meals on board may see a different dashboard than the manager who oversees fuel purchasing. But each manager's customized dashboard also shows which planes are flying where.

Quality-improvement systems Quality-improvement systems come in many different forms, including the following:

- **Plan-Do-Check-Act.** Popularized by total quality management (TQM) founder W. Edwards Deming, the Plan-Do-Check-Act framework helps managers establish a cycle of continuous improvement. The cycle comprises these steps: (1) *Plan*—Identify a performance problem and the processes affecting it; (2) *Do*—Explore potential solutions and implement one; (3) *Check*—Assess how well your solution worked; (4) *Act*—If your solution worked well, institutionalize it and look for another improvement opportunity. If it didn't, return to step 1.

- **Six Sigma.** With roots tracing back to the 1920s, Six Sigma is a data- and measurement-driven approach that helps managers continually improve business processes through reduction of errors. Many companies that use Six Sigma apply it to all their business processes—manufacturing, product development, order fulfillment, customer service, and so forth.

- **Baldrige National Quality Program.** Established in 1987 by a congressional act, the Baldrige National Quality Program was developed by the United States' National Institute of Standards and Technology. (The program is named after Malcolm Baldrige, who served as secretary of commerce from 1981 until 1987.) The Baldrige program defines criteria for high-quality business performance in numerous areas, such as leadership, strategic planning, customer focus, and knowledge management. The Baldrige framework has a European equivalent: the European Foundation for Quality Management. Every year, companies can apply for the Malcolm Baldrige Award, which recognizes organizations for achievement in specific categories: manufacturing, small business, education, and health care.

Balanced Scorecard Introduced in 1992 by Harvard Business School professor Robert Kaplan and David Norton, the head of a management consulting firm, the *Balanced Scorecard* (BSC) system recognizes that financial performance is just one part of the larger picture of organizational performance. The system seeks to balance a company's financial "perspective" with three nonfinancial "perspectives": customer, internal processes, and workforce learning and development. Companies that implement the BSC methodology develop and use two powerful tools.

The first tool is a *strategy map*—a one-page document that graphically depicts executives' theory of the organization's strategy and the cause-and-effect relationships among objectives in the four scorecard perspectives. The map shows the strategic objectives of each perspective and how they will affect performance on objectives in other perspectives. Many companies develop a corporate-level strategy map as well as strategy maps for each division, unit, and department. These lower-level maps contain objectives supporting the high-level map.

The second tool is the *scorecard*, which contains the metrics, targets, and actual performance data for each objective on the strategy map. Companies have a corporate-level scorecard that links down to lower-level business and support-unit scorecards. Organizations often automate their scorecards with special software: when unit managers input data into their scorecards, the data is automatically aggregated into the high-level scorecard to show overall company performance. Software also allows managers to distribute and analyze reports easily.

Adopted by corporations, not-for-profit organizations, and public-sector entities (including government agencies, municipalities, and military forces), the BSC has become widely used for strategy execution.

Which system does your company use? If you don't know whether your organization has adopted a PM system or which system it uses, how do you find out? The quickest way is to ask your manager. In addition, many organizations publish articles about their PM system in company newsletters and refer to it in their annual reports and other publications. In some organizations, an internal performance measurement team provides training on the system to existing employees and new hires.

Look to all these sources for information if necessary. And listen for mention of a particular PM system while attending CEO speeches and all-staff meetings.

Making performance measurement a regular part of your job: three steps Whether or not your organization has adopted a companywide performance measurement system, you can generate important benefits for your business by making performance measurement a regular part of your job. How? When you assess your group's results and uncover the causes behind troubling changes in your results, you can engineer the interventions needed for your group to improve its performance and thus help the company generate better overall results.

How might you use measurement to better manage your group's performance? You first need to understand the performance measurement process. This process consists of three steps, each of which we'll explore in detail in the sections that follow. Here's a brief description of the steps:

In step 1, deciding what to measure, you:

 • **Define your objectives**—for example, "Increase customer satisfaction," "Decrease on-the-job accidents," or "Cut expenses."

 • **Define critical success factors (CSFs)**—the component parts of successfully achieved objectives, in other words, the actions that must be taken collectively to achieve a given objective. For instance, CSFs for the objective "Increase customer satisfaction" might include "Reduce sales staff turnover" and "Improve on-time delivery performance."

 • **Define performance metrics**—the measures you'll use to assess whether you're accomplishing your CSFs. Examples include "Average length of salesperson tenure in department," "Number of sales staff departures per quarter," and "Percentage of orders delivered within +/− six hours of promised delivery time."

In step 2, gathering performance data, you:

• **Set targets for each metric**—for instance, "An 8 percent to 10 percent reduction in sales-staff turnover during the second half of our fiscal year" and "98 percent of orders delivered on time."

• **Collect performance data.** For example, count the number of sales staff who left the company during the final six months of the company's fiscal year, or record the delivery time of all orders during the past quarter.

In step 3, interpreting performance data, you:

• **Analyze performance data.** To illustrate, monitor the number of sales-staff departures that occur each quarter and determine whether you're on track to reduce turnover by 8 percent to 10 percent as planned. In analyzing the data, you'll want to examine the documented reasons for sales-staff departures (such as dismissals, transfers to other departments, acceptance of similar positions at a competitor, or retirements).

- **Test your measurement system.** For instance, ask whether any metrics should be changed to more accurately represent the objective you're trying to achieve, or whether targets have been set at appropriate levels.

Let's now take a look at step 1, deciding what to measure.

Step 1: Deciding What to Measure

I n the first step of the performance measurement process, you decide which aspects of your group's performance you want to measure. You define your *objectives, critical success factors (CSFs),* and *performance metrics.*

If your company uses a formal performance measurement system, senior managers in the organization or the unit supervising the PA system may already have defined one or more of these elements for your group. The performance data you gather must then be in a form that's compatible with the companywide system.

If your organization does not have a formal PA system and you want to track performance on important business activities, you'll need to generate your own objectives, CSFs, and metrics.

Defining your objectives

Your objectives represent what you want to accomplish in order to improve various aspects of your group's performance. To brainstorm ideas for objectives, meet with colleagues and direct reports in your group and ask the following questions:

- **What does our group hope to accomplish by measuring performance?** For instance, does your group hope to identify solutions to recurring problems? Improve overall process efficiency? Determine rewards for particular levels of employee performance?

- **What must our group do to help carry out our company's strategy?** For example, if your company's strategy centers on operational excellence (improving efficiency), you might set objectives for your group such as "Increase sales revenue per employee," "Lower indirect costs," or "Reduce workplace accidents."

- **How might we better serve our customers?** Whether your group serves internal or external customers, think about how you can provide them with greater value. For instance, if you lead an HR group, your objectives might include "Develop future leaders in the organization," "Help managers retain talented employees," and "Foster a collaborative culture." If you lead a product development group, your objectives might include "Increase innovation," "Update products more frequently," and "Make products easier to use."

- **How might we improve our work processes?** Sometimes process problems can be translated into ideas for objectives. For example, suppose you lead a group in the accounting department and your direct reports tend to have difficulty meeting deadlines. In this case, you might define objectives such as "Complete accounts receivable reports on time," "Pay vendors according to their terms," and "Process employee expense reimbursements on schedule."

- **What new skills or knowledge do we need to excel?** Objectives for improving your employees' skills and knowledge might include "Take advantage of more training opportunities," "Improve knowledge sharing," and so forth.

After brainstorming ideas for objectives, review your list and identify the most important ones: those objectives that most directly
affect company and unit strategy or that will help you solve
serious performance problems. Try to whittle your list down to
five to seven objectives.

Defining critical success factors

For each objective in your final list, decide which two or three actions would best enable your group to accomplish that objective.
These become your critical success factors. Table 2 gives some
examples.

Measure what you want, not want what you can measure.
    —Robert S. Kaplan and David P. Norton

TABLE 2

Examples of critical success factors

Objective	Critical success factors
"Reduce workplace accidents"	• "Train employees on proper use of equipment" • "Provide appropriate safety equipment and apparel" • "Regularly inspect workshop for compliance with safety rules"
"Improve knowledge sharing"	• "Improve new-hire mentoring" • "Establish rewards for sharing or accepting new ideas"

Defining performance metrics

Your performance metrics indicate how you'll determine whether you've carried out the critical success factors you've identified and indicate the kind of data you'll need to gather. You can translate each CSF into one or more metrics, as shown in table 3.

TABLE 3

Examples of performance metrics

Critical success factor	Performance metric
"Train employees on proper use of equipment"	• "Number of employees who complete training course with passing grade by end of quarter"
"Establish rewards for sharing or accepting new ideas"	• "Number of new ideas adopted across business units" • "Number of best practices posted to company's knowledge management system"

Tips for defining performance metrics

- **Start with your objectives and critical success factors.** For each objective you define, list two or three actions that would best enable your group to achieve that objective. These actions become your critical success factors. Translate each CSF into one or more performance metrics. For example, the CSF "Improve retention" could be translated into the performance metric "Percentage of new hires who stay beyond their first year."

- **Look beyond financial measures.** Ensure that your set of metrics reflects the nonfinancial as well as the financial aspects of your group's performance. For example, do you have metrics for nonfinancial matters such as process efficiencies, employee knowledge, and customer experiences?

- **Identify cause-and-effect linkages.** Examine your set of metrics for cause-and-effect connections. For example, how will good performance on the metric "Number of order-processing errors" affect performance on the metric "Customer satisfaction" or "Employee morale"? What's the strength of these relationships? For instance, will you need just a small improvement in error reduction to generate a large improvement in customer satisfaction? The more cause-and-effect linkages between your metrics—and the deeper your understanding of the relative strength of these linkages—the more comprehensive a picture you'll have of your group's performance.

- **Examine your lagging/leading mix.** Review your set of metrics. Ask whether they show a mix of lagging (backward-looking) and leading (forward-looking) indicators. Your set of metrics should contain both lagging and leading indicators.

- **Strive for a balance of subjective and objective metrics.** Determine whether your metrics reflect both subjective (such as customer satisfaction) and objective (for example, revenues) indicators. If not, revise your metrics so that they show a mix of these two types of indicators.

- **Consider availability, validity, and reliability of data.** For each metric, ask yourself whether data exists to track performance on that metric, and whether the data will be reliable.

A performance metric is useless if you can't gather the required data or depend on the data to be up-to-date and accurate.

- **Draw on internal and external data.** In addition to analyzing information within your organization (such as sales figures), examine data outside your company (such as third-party rankings of companies' performance against competitors').

- **Use clear, accessible language.** Phrase your performance metrics in specific, concrete, and easy-to-understand language—such as "Number of late deliveries per month" instead of "Service quality."

Evaluating data sources

In defining metrics, the kind of data you'll need and the sources of data you'll use become important considerations. Ask yourself these questions to evaluate your data sources:

- **Where will you get the needed data?** In some cases, your organization may already collect data that you can use— such as employee participation in certain training programs. In other cases, you'll need to gather the data yourself, which may require you to set up new processes and systems. Data may also come from external sources. For example, your company may have hired a vendor to track the number of employees enrolled in benefits programs.

- **How will you gather subjective data?** Performance metrics can require objective *or* subjective data. For example, to track the metric "Percentage increase in sales revenue," you'd gather objective data (changes in sales revenue over a specific period of time). But how would you collect information to track the metric "Percentage increase in customer satisfaction"? In this case, you'd need to gather *subjective* data, such as comments or ratings from customer surveys. Even subjective data must be quantified, for example, expressing customer satisfaction ratings on a scale of 1 to 5 to enable comparison and highlight opportunities for improvement.

- **Should you use composite data?** If you want a big-picture view of your group's performance, consider using metrics that require composite data—data from numerous sources aggregated into one number. Well-known examples include the S&P 500 stock market index and the J.D. Power index of customer satisfaction with new cars and ratings of new-car quality. An example of composite data a company might use to measure performance would be a "brand index," which might combine, say, advertising budget, percentage of target audience reached, and brand impression (what people think of the company's brand, measured in a survey). Because the component measures are dissimilar, they would need to be mathematically adjusted to weight them properly.

- **Will your data be reliable?** While defining metrics, do everything you can to ensure the reliability of the data you'll need to gather. For example, will the data be up to date? Sufficiently detailed? Accurate? Auditable? Will the data be available frequently enough for you to reliably track performance on your metrics?

Step 2: Gathering Performance Data

I n the second step of the performance measurement process, you gather and check the reliability of data on the metrics you've identified. Start this phase by setting targets for each metric you've defined.

Setting targets

Targets represent the performance you want to see on each of your metrics. Table 4 gives examples.

Setting targets is a bit of an art. For example, you want to set targets that inspire people to deliver exceptional performance. But you

TABLE 4

Examples of targets

Performance metric	Target
"Number of employees who complete training course with passing grade by end of quarter"	"All employees complete training course with an end-of-course test score of 80 or above out of a possible 100 by end of quarter"
"Percentage of existing products updated with new features midway through the fiscal year"	"85% of existing products updated"
"Customer satisfaction index"	"Achieve 85% of customers who are very satisfied or extremely satisfied, which represents a 15% increase in customer satisfaction by year end"

don't want to set targets so high that your direct reports assume they can't reach them—and so don't bother trying. In addition, you have to figure out what constitutes reasonable targets.

For instance, if you're aiming for a defect rate of 100 parts per million (PPM) in a process your group performs, but industry defect rates for a similar process currently range from 400 to 1,000 PPM, your target may be unrealistic.

Tips for setting performance targets

- **Establish a three-point range of targets for your metrics.** These three types of targets can work together to shape your group's future performance. For example, a minimum target of "12 percent error rate" can feel more manageable to employees and help them gain the positive results and confidence to meet your moderate ("9 percent error rate") and even "stretch" ("4 percent error rate") targets.
- **Involve your employees.** Your direct reports are closest to the action and in the best position to provide information on what's possible in their work. Involve them in setting targets; you'll gain their buy-in as they feel a sense of ownership in the process.
- **Consider trends to establish a target baseline.** If past data exists for performance on a particular metric, examine that data for trends that can serve as a baseline for setting targets for future performance. For example, suppose you want to set a target for employee turnover over the coming six months, and turnover rates for your group have climbed slowly from 2 percent to 7 percent over the previous two years. In this case,

a target of reducing turnover from 7 percent to 4 percent in the next six months may make sense and be realistic.

- **Get your boss's input.** Ask your boss for ideas about what level of performance on each metric might best enable your group to achieve its objectives. Your boss may have some helpful suggestions based on his or her experience and understanding of unit and company goals.

- **Use SWOT analysis.** Consider your group's internal *strengths* and *weaknesses,* as well as its external *opportunities* and *threats*. Ask yourself what targets would enable your group to build on its strengths and leverage opportunities, as well as minimize weaknesses and threats. For instance, if your group is particularly knowledgeable about your company's products, perhaps the ambitious target of "25 percent increase in customer loyalty by quarter end" is perfectly realistic and achievable.

- **Gather feedback from customers and other stakeholders.** Expectations from these groups might yield insights you can use to set targets. For example, by asking customers what constitutes great performance in their minds, you can generate targets that will meet or even exceed their performance requirements.

- **Consider industry averages.** Numerous credible agencies monitor performance of specific industries; for example, J.D. Power & Associates tracks many industries. Review these performance ratings, and decide whether they can inform your targets. For instance, if error rates in an industrywide manufacturing process that your company uses range from 5 percent to 10 percent, those figures may serve as a reasonable target for your error-rate metrics.

- **Identify initiatives.** While considering targets, ask yourself what new projects or change efforts may be required to support achieving your targets. For example, to meet a target of "100 percent on-time delivery of orders," will your employees need a new software application to track fulfillment processes? Will they need training on the new system?

Using benchmarking and baselines

How do you deal with the challenge of setting targets? Benchmarking can help. Use information from trade associations, industry publications, the Internet, and outside sources to *benchmark*, or compare your performance data and metrics with those of other companies. Some are very well known—such as the J.D. Power rankings. Also consider internal benchmarking sources—such as performance data from other groups that carry out similar processes or that have goals similar to yours. Then set targets that seem reasonable in light of the benchmarking information you've gathered.

Baselines, or starting points, can also help. If you're setting targets for a performance metric on which your group or company has already gathered actual data, it can be helpful to use that data to establish a baseline. Many managers use the current period's results or a yearly average to set their targets. For example, if your group's sales have increased an average of 5 percent every quarter over the past two years, you might consider setting a target sales increase of 6 percent or 8 percent per quarter for the coming year.

For metrics on which no data exists, you might research an industry average and use that as your baseline.

Note: Using past data to set a baseline for your targets can be tricky. After all, how do you decide which number should serve as your reference point? For example, suppose you want to use sales from the fourth quarter of last year as your baseline. How confident can you be that the fourth-quarter figure represents a useful average of your group's performance? If there were unusual circumstances during that quarter (such as a large number of unfilled sales positions), the figure may not be a good reference point, because sales would be lower than usual.

For these reasons, it's important to carefully evaluate the historical data you're considering using as your target baseline. Look at how the data for a particular period compares with the data from preceding evaluation periods to see whether there has been an abrupt change from the previous performance. If there has been, you'll want to investigate the reasons for the change by asking your boss and peer managers for insights. And you may want to consider using a different period's data to inform your target.

Determining a target range

Many managers set a three-point (minimum, moderate, and "stretch") range for certain targets. For example, for the performance metric "Increase sales," the minimum target might be "$500,000 sales per quarter"; the moderate target, "$800,000 sales per quarter"; the "stretch" target, "$1 million sales per quarter."

This approach offers several advantages. Minimum targets can feel more manageable to employees and help them see what progress they need to make in order to reach the moderate and stretch goals. Though minimum targets aren't truly subpar, managers don't want employees to stop at achieving these targets. The "real" goal is usually the moderate point in the target range.

The "stretch" point in a target range represents the most ambitious target of all. In determining stretch targets, you need to achieve the delicate balance between challenging your employees and being realistic. A stretch target is intended to "raise the bar" enough to get your employees' competitive juices flowing or to stoke their desire for achievement. And it usually requires significant effort to achieve. But it also must be set at a level at which your direct reports have the skills, knowledge, and company resources (equipment, processes, workspace, time) required to meet the target.

Stretch point *n* 1: the point in a target range representing the most ambitious target of all

---

To set stretch targets, make sure you're familiar with your employees' capacities and abilities. How have they reacted in the past when presented with ambitious challenges? Ask yourself how much of a stretch will motivate them to outdo themselves without becoming overwhelmed or demoralized. Also consider whether stretch targets carry the risk of encouraging negative or unethical behavior, such as "gaming" the system to achieve the desired performance. Finally, show your employees how achieving the stretch target on one metric will lead to outstanding performance on another and generate valuable rewards. For example, "If we increase customer loyalty by 10 percent, that will translate into a 15 percent jump in profitability. And that means a boost in your bonus compensation."

Collecting and communicating data

After setting targets, you and/or your direct reports need to begin gathering performance data so you can compare actual performance with your target performance. Data can come from a number of sources. For instance, you may ask people in your department who lead call-center teams to track the number of phone calls customers must make before representatives resolve their complaints or questions.

You may also depend on people in other groups or units to gather data on your performance metrics. Many companies identify "metric owners," who have specific knowledge that enables them to collect valid data on a performance metric. To illustrate, perhaps someone in the HR department will supply data on the number of employees in your group who have attended safety-training courses and passed the end-of-course test. Or the finance manager can give you interim profitability numbers.

How'm I doing?
   —Ed Koch, former mayor of New York City

If your company has a formal performance measurement system in place, senior managers or a dedicated unit may have created data-gathering forms for you and other managers to use. These may be hard-copy documents, such as memos that you fill in by hand and submit to a PA system administrator. Or they may consist of electronic forms—spreadsheets or Web-based data-entry forms that you fill in online and e-mail to the PA system administrator.

Automated data-gathering systems, often linked to a company's data warehouse or enterprise resource planning system, offer numerous benefits. They handle huge volumes of data easily and can generate reports showing the data in different formats (such as pie charts, tables, or graphs). In addition, they can aggregate data from different units or groups into one number. For instance, the system may show "Division sales," while also enabling managers to drill down to see sales generated by each region and salesperson within the division. They also help you analyze cause and effect by enabling you to "slice and dice" data in different ways.

If your organization doesn't use a formal performance measurement system, you may need to develop data-gathering forms yourself. In this case, simplicity and ease of use are critical to getting the data you need. Develop a consistent form that enables you and other metric owners to provide information easily, conveniently, and quickly, and that accommodates short notes regarding the data. Table 5 gives an example of a simple, easy-to-use data-gathering form for the metric "Percentage of one-call resolutions":

TABLE 5

Data-gathering form

Metric	Target	Performance data			Notes
		July	Aug.	Sept.	
"Percentage of one-call resolutions"	75% per month	55%	65%	55%	September data is misleading. The percentage of one-call resolutions logged that month fell far short of the target, but that's because during the peak summer vacation period, we were short-staffed and had to hire temps who were less knowledgeable.

Steps for communicating performance data to your group

1. **Review your group's performance data.** Gather all the reports, forms, and other documents in which your group's performance data is recorded for the period in question. Review the data, looking for places where actual performance differs from the targets you set.

2. **Craft a story about what's happening.** Based on what you're seeing in your group's performance data, develop a narrative describing what's happening with performance. Highlight interrelationships between metrics, and note possible explanations for why actual performance is differing from targeted performance—for example, "We're having trouble reaching our targeted 3 percent error rate, and that's negatively affecting customer satisfaction and costs. New hires and order-processing software may have played a part in raising the error rate these past two months." Seek others' ideas about the underlying causes of performance problems. Peer managers, your boss, and some of your employees may have valuable insights into what's going on.

3. **Create charts and graphs.** Where possible, translate numerical information into simple charts and graphs that capture trends. For example, a line graph showing an increase in error rate over the past six months can prove far more compelling than a list of numbers. Also, snapshot views are handy for senior managers. Thus, if you will be sharing performance results with them, they will appreciate receiving information in such a succinct way.

4. **Select the appropriate degree of detail.** Consider what your employees need to know about the group's performance in order to make improvements. Decide whether the story you've crafted and the charts and graphs you've prepared contain the right degree of detail to make your point. Too much detail, and your employees may become confused or lose interest. Too little detail, and they may not grasp the importance of a performance problem.

5. **Communicate difficult facts constructively.** Even if your narrative, your charts and graphs, and the details you've gathered about your group's performance present a discouraging picture, it's important to communicate the truth about performance to your employees. However, in communicating the information, strive to do so constructively. That is, don't single out individuals as the cause behind poor group performance. Instead, look for the problematic processes and systems behind the shortfalls and explore ideas for addressing them.

6. **Create opportunities for review and discussion.** Set up meetings and review sessions with your group to specifically discuss performance results and changes made to address them. Together, explore what has worked well and what hasn't. Encourage your employees to adopt a mind-set of continual, collective improvement.

Step 3: Interpreting Performance Data

I n the next step of the performance measurement process, you analyze the data you've gathered on your performance metrics and determine its implications. Interpreting performance data is a complex discipline in itself. In many companies, a unit staffed by experts trained in statistical analysis, correlation and regression analysis, and other data-interpretation approaches and tools performs this activity.

But in the interest of gaining an overview of the entire performance measurement process, it's helpful to know a bit about how performance data is evaluated and what you and others might look for when interpreting results.

Comparing targeted and actual performance

You've been gathering data on your performance metrics for some time. What should you do with the data? What do the numbers mean? A good first step is to compare your data with the targets you set for each metric. For example, suppose you set the target, "5 percent maximum product manufacturing error rate," to be reached at the end of six months. You've tracked *actual* error rates over the past six months and recorded the rates (see figure 2).

Clearly, the error rate has fluctuated over the period in question, with a general downward trend. And the rate at the end of the six months is not as low as the 5 percent you set as your target. How should you respond? You might draw several conclusions:

FIGURE 2

Track of actual error rates

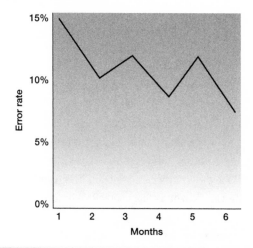

- "We didn't reach our target, so we should overhaul our error-reduction efforts. Perhaps we need a new initiative focused on sharpening shop-floor staff training in using the manufacturing equipment."

- "The trend is generally downward. Even if we didn't reach our target by the end of the six months, we seem to be heading in the right direction. Let's see what happens over the next few months, and decide whether we need to reexamine our error-reduction efforts."

- "The target was too aggressive. We don't have the capacity to reduce errors as much as we had hoped. Let's revise

What Would YOU Do?

On Target with Target Setting?

ALLEN LEADS a product development group in the electronics unit of Hainsworth & Smith, a large consumer goods company. Top management has asked leaders in each business unit to form a special team charged with defining new performance metrics for their unit. Allen's boss has asked him to participate in the electronics unit's team. This team also includes representatives from other functions within the unit, such as manufacturing, operations, finance, and IT. All teams will share their ideas with an executive steering committee, which will then combine the ideas to build the most appropriate companywide performance measurement system.

Hainsworth & Smith's strategy centers on building a global reputation as a company on the leading edge of technology. Several members of the team meet with managers throughout the unit to get their thoughts about the electronics unit's role in executing this strategy.

The team then develops several objectives for the unit that support this strategy, including "Boost rate of successful innovations introduced," "Develop more innovative products for mobile use," and "Speed products to market." The team then defines a few CSFs for each objective and translates the CSFs into performance metrics. Members share the list of metrics with the steering committee, which approves them as a good starting point. They then turn to setting targets for each metric. Members discuss several possibilities. For example, perhaps setting only aggressive targets would stimulate employees' competitive spirit. Or maybe it's more important to maintain employees' confidence by setting flexible targets that can be lowered if they prove unachievable. Allen and the others are struggling with the target-setting process.

What would YOU do? The mentor will suggest a solution in *What You COULD Do.*

---

the target to make it less aggressive—say, a 9 percent error rate."

- "Perhaps the data isn't reliable. How do we know we can trust these rates?"

Given all these possible interpretations, how do you select the best response to what you're seeing in your data?

Deciding how to respond

Savvy managers consider the following four practices for deciding how to respond to performance data:

- **Look for trends** that can help you identify the bigger picture of how performance is changing over time, as reflected in the data you're gathering. If your actual performance is trending in the desired direction, you may not need to intervene.

- **Consider the inherent variability in the process being measured,** so you keep your perspective. You don't want to overreact to a variation in performance measures that is due to normal fluctuations. For example, sales on a particular line of products may vary across seasons. Some companies set ranges of normal variation for such metrics and respond only when actual performance is outside that range.

- **Think about what's causing any variations in the data** that can shed light on the forces beneath variations. Ask yourself what events or forces might underlie the variations you're seeing in your performance data. For instance, suppose you see a major jump in error rates during month three of your data-tracking period. You'd want to investigate what was going on during that time that might have affected the error rate. Was a new piece of manufacturing equipment introduced at that time, and did the production staff have difficulty using it? Maybe the shop floor took on several new hires that month, and they hadn't yet mastered use of the equipment. In each of these cases, you might decide to hold off taking drastic action.

- **Ask whether your targets or metrics need to be changed,** so you can determine if you need to reconsider your targets or metrics. Sometimes, when you see an abrupt change in your performance data, it's a signal that you need to reconsider your targets or metrics. Such signals can occur if your organization has changed an important process. An abrupt change in error rate may, for example, result from an employee scheduling change. Perhaps after starting your measurement program, you stopped the practice of allowing employees to vary their shifts, assigning each person a permanent shift. That could cause error rates to drop and then stabilize, suggesting that you can reasonably set lower targets for that metric.

Here's another example. Suppose that over the past twelve months, you've been tracking the number of weeks it takes to fill vacant positions in your group, with the goal of bringing new hires on board faster. At month six, the number of weeks decreases sharply—and stays at roughly the same level during months seven through twelve. When you investigate, you discover that your company's HR department overhauled its recruiting processes during month six by installing an online job-posting and job-application module in its human resource information system. This new technology has vastly accelerated the hiring process, so that many new hires can now take days instead of weeks. Suddenly, your metric "Number of weeks" has less meaning than it did before. If you still want to accelerate the hiring process, you might change your metric to "Number of days." Or you may decide that the new technology has helped you improve the hiring process sufficiently, and you now want to measure some other aspect of your group's performance.

Clearly, interpreting performance data can be complex and challenging. Your company may have a unit devoted to analyzing all performance data. If it doesn't, and if you're struggling to make sense of a particular set of data, seek help from your boss or from an expert in your company who specializes in statistical analysis.

What You COULD Do

Remember Allen and his team's uncertainty
about how to set targets for their unit's
performance metrics?

Here's what the mentor suggests:

Though aggressive targets can inspire people to deliver exceptional performance, such targets on their own can demoralize people if they're unrealistic. For example, if industry benchmarks show
that product development times typically range from twenty-four
to twenty-seven months, Allen wouldn't want to set a target to
launch new products in twelve months. Given the industry's current
best practice, employees would likely view a 50 percent reduction in
product launch time as an unrealistic target. Any attempt to reach
this target may be marked by discouragement and end in failure.

Moreover, Allen and his team should avoid lowering targets
when actual performance falls short of the target. This approach
misses the point of performance measurement. There will be
times when a target will turn out to be too aggressive and unrealistic, and thus lowers merit. But more often, a better move is to
identify and implement reasonable adjustments to processes, systems, and other aspects of a group's activities to bring actual performance up to the desired levels.

Allen's team should set a range of targets. This will help motivate employees by showing them the gains they need to achieve in

order to boost performance dramatically. In a three-point target range, the "moderate" (midpoint) target represents performance that is slightly beyond what the group can achieve by continuing historical trends. It's achievable if people work together and contribute new ideas about how to achieve the moderate point. The moderate target is augmented by two additional targets: a minimum expectation for improvement over current levels, and an aggressive "stretch" target that lies somewhat beyond what now seems achievable. Stretch targets, if achieved, would represent a dramatic improvement in performance in the eyes of customers and other stakeholders.

Avoiding Common Mistakes

Managers who measure performance routinely encounter common pitfalls during each step in the process. To avoid these pitfalls, start by understanding them. Next, we present seven common mistakes and offer ideas for escaping them.

Too few or too many metrics

Avoid relying on just one metric to measure your group's overall performance. Also resist any urge to create a long list of metrics to measure everything you can think of that relates to your group's performance. The goal is to identify the activities that will have the greatest direct impact on your group's performance and develop metrics for those activities.

If you've defined three or four major objectives for your group, each of those will likely be translated into two or three critical success factors. Each CSF, in turn, will be translated into one or more performance metrics. Thus, four objectives may ultimately translate into as many as twenty-four metrics. If the number of metrics grows much larger than this, you'll expend too much energy tracking data and will lose the "big picture."

Unaligned metrics

Ensure that the objectives and metrics you define support your company's and unit's strategic goals. Too many managers decide to measure aspects of their group's performance that have little connection to higher-level goals. For example, a call-center manager might take a keen interest in his group's ability to process customer phone calls quickly. The manager tells his employees that he's measuring how quickly they process and complete calls and bases their performance evaluations on this metric. You can be certain that employees will work hard to get callers off the line promptly. But if the company has defined a strategy involving cross-selling, hustling callers off the phone as fast as possible could easily undermine the corporate strategy.

Overly aggressive targets

It's tempting to think that setting aggressive "stretch" targets for your metrics will get your employees' competitive juices flowing and generate unprecedented performance. While that's a possibility, aggressive targets can also demoralize your employees if they lack the resources to meet the targets and if they view the targets as unreachable and unrealistic. You want to set targets high enough to inspire your direct reports to reach for better performance, but not so high that employees conclude they can't possibly reach them.

Setting overly aggressive targets can backfire in another way—by motivating unethical, possibly even illegal, behavior. For example, tough sales and revenue targets have led to serious problems in the insurance industry, resulting in a federal investigation of company practices.

Manipulation of performance data

A company's or unit's selection of metrics can sometimes lead managers to "game" the system in order to meet the targeted performance.

For example, consider a car company that aims to be "the best-rated customer service car company in the industry." This company will have metrics related to customer satisfaction, customer loyalty, and the number of customer complaints. New-car salespeople who work in this company know that their compensation depends on what customers write on the feedback forms that corporate headquarters sends them after a sale. Immediately after closing a deal, salespeople may "coach" the customer on how to fill out the form. They may even appeal to the customer's compassion: "My income depends on what you say on the form. I hope you'll help me." Result? Annoyed customers who feel manipulated by desperate salespeople—and a lack of valid feedback to the company about its salespeople's performance.

Here are additional examples: your direct reports (or even your peers in other departments) may purposely low-ball targets so they can easily exceed them and get bonus compensation and recognition. Or a sales team leader may exaggerate the tough selling environment so you'll set low sales targets and he can look like a star performer without having to work too hard.

The lesson? Measurement systems can change employees' behaviors, sometimes in ways a company never intended! Avoid this scenario in your own group by making sure to do the following before you set targets:

- Take time to find out how your people might be altering their behaviors in order to meet targets you've set for the performance metrics you're using.

- Consider whether these behavior changes might be causing unintended—and unwanted—consequences for your group and your company.

- If you ask some of your direct reports to provide input on target setting, try to verify the rationale behind their suggestions. Don't just take them at their word; ask them what sources they're using to form their opinions about targets, and verify the reliability of those sources.

Difficulty validating data

Validating data means assessing its accuracy and reliability. Some data—such as revenues or expenses—is easily validated because it's objective and regularly audited. For example, you can tabulate invoices generated by your group to determine whether the revenue figures for your group are correct. Or you can review accounts payable figures to judge the accuracy of expense information. Data provided by outside sources—such as organizations that track companies' market share—can also be considered valid.

Other data is more difficult to validate. Consider employee morale, a new product's innovativeness, and customer satisfaction. Such things may be important indicators of your group's performance. But how reliable is the data you gather on these metrics? Because such data is subjective, it can be easily manipulated by individuals seeking to make their performance look better than it really is. Still, subjective data is important. In fact, leading indicators are often predominantly subjective (customer surveys and employee morale, for example) and are valuable because they can help your organization proactively manage performance. However, avoid relying on just one subjective metric as the indicator for a critical success factor. A single subjective metric won't give you a comprehensive enough picture of what's going on.

Inappropriate responses to performance shortfalls

When you see actual performance data that falls far short of your target performance, avoid the following inappropriate responses:

- **Knee-jerk interventions.** Don't overreact to every performance shortfall. You might intervene too quickly—such as by firing someone, or by launching a large-scale, expensive change initiative that doesn't address the real reasons behind the shortfall. Instead, take time to investigate what may have caused the performance shortfall and to consider a range of possible solutions to the problem.

- **Lowering your targets.** The simplest way to close gaps between targeted and actual performance is to lower your targets so they're easier to reach next time around. But that approach misses the point of performance measurement. Sometimes a target may in fact be too aggressive and merit revision. But in other cases, the more appropriate response is to identify reasonable changes in processes, organizational structures, and other aspects of your group to bring actual performance up to targeted performance.

Outdated objectives and measures

Things change. The economy shifts. New competitors emerge. Your company or unit modifies its strategy. Your customer base changes. Technology advances. What was significant to your company's success three years ago may no longer be significant today.

Your performance objectives and metrics need to be relevant to current business conditions, yet you also want to keep metrics as consistent as possible over time so you can compare historical performance. The solution? Regularly assess changes in your external and internal environment. And strive to maintain a balance: keep objectives and metrics consistent where possible and appropriate, modifying them only if necessary to reflect changing realities.

Avoiding the pitfalls described is critical to accurately appraising your group's performance. When you collect data that truly reflects what's going on in your group, you can more effectively *manage* your own and your employees' performance.

Maura's Story

B y *measuring* your group's performance, you ultimately
manage that performance more effectively. In other words,
by pulling away from your daily routine and thinking carefully
about how your group does what it does, you can determine how
effectively your group is operating. You can then address shortfalls
and other problems, whether they stem from your direct reports'
performance, your managing style, or some other source.

Consider the following story about Maura, who heads up a
large sales group. Through the process of appraising her group's
performance, she makes some insightful discoveries that help her
manage her group more effectively.

Setting objectives, CSFs, and metrics

Maura was recently promoted to manager of a large sales group.
Her company does not use a formal performance measurement
system, so she and her boss work together to define objectives
for her group. Because the company has defined a strategy for en-
hancing profitability and market share, Maura and her boss select
several objectives—including increasing customer satisfaction,
improving sales staff morale, and boosting sales revenues—that
support those high-level goals.

Maura also defines critical success factors for each of her
group's objectives. For example, her CSFs for increasing customer

satisfaction include "Reduce sales staff turnover," "Improve sales staff responsiveness," and "Reduce order-processing errors."

For many of Maura's objectives, reducing sales-staff turnover is a CSF. As Maura explains to her boss:

- If turnover increases, customers become uneasy because the sales reps they've come to know are no longer available to them. Worried customers may start taking their business elsewhere.

- Turnover also affects morale among sales reps who remain with the company. If more sales staff start leaving, those who remain may start asking themselves why so many of their former colleagues have defected. They may decide to leave as well, further worsening turnover.

- Turnover burdens remaining reps with larger workloads, because it takes time to hire new reps to replace the defectors. Struggling under heavy loads, remaining reps may have difficulty closing deals, thus reducing the company's revenues.

After defining CSFs for each of her objectives, Maura translates them into metrics. For instance, her metric for sales-staff turnover is "Percentage annual turnover in sales staff." Other metrics include "Revenue per sales staff," "Number of order-processing errors," "Customer loyalty," and "Number of calls required to resolve customer complaints and questions."

Gathering performance data

Maura next sets targets for each of the metrics she has defined. She and her boss think carefully about the targets. For example, Maura knows that she can't eliminate turnover entirely in her group. But she wants to keep it at a minimum. She benchmarks sales-staff turnover in other, similar companies, as well as in other customer-facing groups within her organization. After reviewing the information, she decides that a target of 5 percent annual turnover is reasonable and will help her achieve her objectives. She uses a similar process to set targets for her remaining metrics.

Maura then begins gathering performance data on all the metrics she has defined and compares the data to her targets. For instance, she starts tracking the number of sales reps who leave the company each month and calculating how that rate compares with the 5 percent annual turnover rate she had set as her target. She figures her target is a monthly average rate of 0.4 percent (0.4 percent $\times$ 12 = 5 percent annually).

In gathering and reviewing performance data, Maura sees some disturbing developments. In particular, turnover in her group is trending upward. Over the six months that Maura has been measuring performance, monthly turnover rates have slowly climbed from 0.4 percent to 0.5 percent. Turnover for the current month has already reached 0.7 percent, and there are still two weeks remaining in the month. In addition, increasing turnover has clearly begun to hurt customer satisfaction and revenues, just as Maura had feared. Performance on the metrics she defined for those objectives has fallen far short of the targets she set.

Maura knows she must investigate and address the causes behind these performance shortfalls.

Interpreting performance data

Maura sets out to interpret the performance data she's seeing to determine what it's telling her and how she might intervene. For example, to investigate increasing turnover rates, Maura takes the following steps:

- **She looks for trends.** For instance, she asks herself whether sales rep departures demonstrate any patterns, such as increasing sharply just after quarterly bonuses are paid.

- **She considers historical context.** Maura asks the HR department what the turnover rates have been in her group for several years before she came on board.

- **She identifies underlying themes in the reasons behind defections.** For example, do most of the sales reps who leave go to work for a particular competitor? Are many of them making career changes? Have they expressed dissatisfaction with certain aspects of the company or her leadership? Has the company announced plans for a merger or acquisition, or plans to discontinue a product line that might mean sales force layoffs?

- **She compares her group's turnover to that of other groups.** For instance, are other customer-facing groups experiencing similar turnover rates? What about industry averages?

Making important discoveries

Through this process, Maura makes several discoveries. For one thing, she finds that her group has been experiencing higher turnover rates than other customer-facing groups in the company. She also determines that turnover has increased steadily since she began leading the group. Equally troubling, she learns that departing sales reps' exit interviews contain a preponderance of comments about her "unavailability."

As painful as these realizations are, they enable Maura to design and implement solutions to the turnover problem. For example, she begins holding more frequent meetings with sales reps and getting to know more about their career interests. She also has lunch with several peer managers and asks them how they control turnover in their sales groups. She adopts some of their suggestions. These include responding more quickly to phone calls and e-mails from sales reps who need help resolving problems or who want to explore ideas for better serving customers.

Maura's efforts pay off: over the next two quarters, turnover in her group levels off. During the following quarter, it even begins to decline. Customer satisfaction rates start improving, and revenues for her group begin to pick up.

By *appraising* her group's performance, Maura has discovered how to better *manage* that performance. As a result, she has begun generating more value for her company and its customers—and is helping her organization achieve its strategic goals.

Tips and Tools

Tools for Measuring Performance

Worksheet for Understanding Key Performance Indicators

Use this worksheet to identify and understand your company's and unit's key performance indicators (KPIs).

1. What are your company's high-level goals? *Consider the type of organization you work for, its mission, and its strategy. For example, if your company is global, perhaps a high-level goal is to expand sales in international markets. If your organization is a social service nonprofit, maybe a goal is to reduce the ratio of administrative costs to total donations received. If you're not sure of your company's high-level goals, ask your boss for clarification.*

2. What measures does your company use to assess how well it's achieving its high-level goals? *These measures are the company's key performance indicators. Examples may include "Percentage of income deriving from international markets," "Total administrative costs as a percentage of donations received," "Return on investment," "Economic value added," and "Break-even time." If you're not sure which KPIs your company uses, ask your boss for advice. Most companies have three or four KPIs.*

3. Of your company's key performance indicators, which are input KPIs? Which are process KPIs? And which are output KPIs? *Input KPIs might include investments in research and development, funding for employee training, quality of raw materials, and other assets and resources used to generate business results. Process KPIs might encompass order delivery time, time to fill vacant positions, product repair cycle time, and other efficiency-related measurements. Output KPIs might include revenues, return on investment, economic value added, break-even time, revenues, number of new customers, and other results of business activities.*

4. What KPIs has your unit defined? *Each unit has different KPIs tailored to its function within the company. For instance, the customer service department probably tracks the*

number of customers served during a given time period. The product development unit likely assesses the number of new offerings introduced and the ratio of new to existing products. And the human resources unit probably measures workforce skill levels, hiring efficiency, and other human capital–related activities.

5. Which of your unit's KPIs are input? Process? Output? *See the examples in question 3 for reminders.*

6. In what ways do your unit's KPIs relate to and support your company's KPIs? *For example, suppose you work for a global consumer goods company that has a KPI "Percentage of income deriving from international markets," and you lead a group in the adult apparel unit. In this case, your unit's KPIs might include "Number of satellite offices established in Europe," "Total sales for Europe, Middle East/Africa, and Asia," and other KPIs related to your company's goals.*

Worksheet for Understanding Your Company's Performance Measurement System

Use this worksheet to identify and understand the performance measurement approach your company uses.

1. What aspects of business performance does your company measure? *For example, does it measure improvements in all business processes (manufacturing, product development, order fulfillment, customer service), or just some—and if so, which ones? Does it assess the effectiveness of solutions to problems? Does it look beyond financial indicators to assess nonfinancial "perspectives" on business performance such as workforce learning, process efficiency, and customer service? Does it track performance on criteria such as knowledge management, customer focus, leadership quality, and strategic planning? If you're not sure, talk with someone in the unit or team responsible for measuring performance.*

2. What kinds of performance data does your unit routinely gather? And how is this data used to help form a picture of overall company performance? *If you're unsure, ask your boss for his or her insight.*

3. Has your company adopted a formal performance measurement (PM) system? If so, what is it? *Common PM systems include a dashboard or cockpit, as well as quality-improvement systems such as Plan-Do-Check-Act, Six Sigma, and the Baldrige National Quality Program. The Balanced Scorecard is another widely used performance measurement system; many companies use it to understand the relationship among nonfinancial performance and financial results, and to better manage strategy execution. If you're not sure whether your company uses a formal PM system or which system it uses, ask your supervisor for clarification.*

4. How is performance data from each unit in your company entered into the company's PM system? *Do unit managers collect data from group leaders such as yourself, aggregate the data on spreadsheets, and e-mail the documents to the PM system team? Is*

there an internal Web site that unit managers can use to input the aggregated performance data?

5. What kinds of performance reports does your company's PM system generate? *Does the system produce monthly or quarterly company-level results broken down by unit? Are results coded in some way to indicate how they compare with performance targets? For example, do reports use a "traffic light" system—coding on-target or above-target performance as green and problem performance as yellow or red?*

6. How does your unit use the performance information generated by the company's PM system? *Who has access to the information? Do unit leaders such as your boss meet regularly with group leaders to discuss performance results?*

Worksheet for Deciding Which Performance Aspects to Measure

Use this tool to define objectives for your group, identify critical success factors (CSFs) for each objective, and translate your CSFs into performance metrics. This tool is especially helpful if your company does not use a formal performance measurement system.

1. What does your group need to achieve in order to contribute to your company's performance? *Consider ways in which your group can support your unit's or company's strategy, solve recurring business problems, serve customers better, and acquire needed skills or knowledge. Brainstorm as many ideas as you can.*

2. Of the needed achievements you listed in step 1, which do you consider *most* important? Why? *Try to whittle your list down to about five to seven items. These become your group's objectives.*

3. Look at each objective you listed in step 2. For each objective, identify the two or three actions that would best enable your group to accomplish that objective. *These become your critical success factors (CSFs). For example, if one of your objectives is "Improve knowledge sharing," your CSFs might include "Improve new-hire mentoring" and "Establish job-shadowing relationships." Note your ideas in the table below. Ask your employees or colleagues for ideas, too—the people closest to each process or task can often provide helpful insights.*

Objective	Critical Success Factors

4. Look again at each CSF you listed in step 3. Express each CSF as one or more performance metrics. *For instance, the CSF "Improve new-hire mentoring" could be translated into the performance metrics "Percentage of new hires this year who have mentors assigned by their start date" and "New hires' knowledge of company policies and job responsibilities." List each CSF and its corresponding performance metric(s) in the table below.*

Objective 1:	
Critical Success Factor	**Corresponding Performance Metric(s)**
Objective 2:	
Critical Success Factor	**Corresponding Performance Metric(s)**
Objective 3:	
Critical Success Factor	**Corresponding Performance Metric(s)**
Objective 4:	
Critical Success Factor	**Corresponding Performance Metric(s)**

Objective 5:	
Critical Success Factor	**Corresponding Performance Metric(s)**

Objective 6:	
Critical Success Factor	**Corresponding Performance Metric(s)**

Objective 7:	
Critical Success Factor	**Corresponding Performance Metric(s)**

5. Document your ideas about how you'll gather the data required to track the performance metrics you've defined in step 4. *For each metric, list ideas for gathering the data in the table below.*

Metric	Possible Data Sources
Example:	**Example:**
"Number of employees who pass training with an end-of-course score of 80 out of 100"	*HR department or consultancy that provided the training*

Worksheet for Setting Performance Targets

*Use this tool to set performance targets for the metrics that you've created for your
group or that your boss has defined for your group based on the company's
formal performance measurement system.*

- In the first column of the table below, list the performance metrics established for your group.
- In the second column, write a range of possible targets.
- In the third column, note your rationale for the target ranges you're proposing. Possible influences on your choice of target may include benchmarks (such as targets considered reasonable by other companies in your industry) as well as historical data that can serve as a baseline for your target.

Metric	Possible Targets	Rationale
Example:	*Example:*	*Example:*
Percentage increase in customer satisfaction by year end	*Minimum: 5%* *Moderate: 8%* *Stretch: 10% increase in customer satisfaction by year end*	*10% is a bit aggressive but may stimulate my group's competitive spirit. We have the systems, skills, and commitment in place to push for this stretch target. Also, over the past year, customer satisfaction picked up during the third and fourth quarters. I think we've got some momentum going that we can use to achieve these increases.*

Worksheet for Tracking Performance Results

Use this tool to track your group's performance results over several evaluation periods and to document thoughts about how to interpret and respond to the results.

- In the first column in the table below, list the performance metrics established for your group.
- In the second column, record the target you've set for each metric.
- In the next three columns, record the actual performance for each metric over each evaluation period.
- In the final column, record your thoughts about what the performance data seems to be indicating and how you might best respond to the data.

Metric	Target	Performance Data			Notes
Example: % of one-call resolutions of customer complaints	*Example:* 75% per month	*Example:* Jan. 55%	*Example:* Feb. 65%	*Example:* Mar. 55%	*Example:* Investigate drop in performance during March. Possible causes: we were short-staffed because several people were out on vacation; installed new phone system that some people had difficulty learning to use.

Test Yourself

This section offers ten multiple-choice questions to help you identify your baseline knowledge of the essentials of measuring performance.

Answers to the questions are given at the end of the test.

1. What is performance measurement?

  a. Assessing business results to determine a company's effectiveness and to address performance shortfalls and process problems.

  b. Automating performance data collection and reporting so that managers can more quickly assess their group's effectiveness and identify performance problems.

  c. Setting ambitious targets for every employee in a group so that people feel motivated to deliver their best performance possible on the job.

2. What is a key performance indicator?

  a. A measure indicating an individual manager's ability to effectively lead his or her group.

  b. A measure reflecting how an organization is doing in a specific aspect of its performance.

c. A measure representing a company's overall standing in its industry compared with rivals.

3. What is a performance measurement system?

a. A series of graphs showing changes in a company's performance over a specified period.

b. A centralized database containing performance data from every part of an organization.

c. A set of strategic objectives and performance metrics applied throughout an entire enterprise.

4. Which of the following describes the phases of the performance measurement process?

a. Designing reward programs and allocating incentives to a company's business units.

b. Deciding what to measure, gathering performance data, and interpreting performance data.

c. Selecting a formal performance measurement system, implementing it, and updating it.

5. Which of the following phrases represents a performance metric?

a. "Improve knowledge sharing."

b. "100 percent on-time deliveries by end of the fiscal year."

c. "Number of employees who complete training with passing grade by end of quarter."

6. Which of the following would be a strategy for ensuring that you gather valid performance data on the metrics you've created?

a. Accumulate data that is up to date and available frequently enough for you to track performance over time.

b. Collect data yourself on your group's performance, or have your employees collect the data as they perform their work.

c. Gather only objective data—that which can be measured easily—such as sales revenue, costs, and number of new hires.

7. You want to set a target for your metric "Percentage of orders delivered on time." Which of the following approaches would you use?

a. Establish a highly ambitious target—99 percent or 100 percent of orders delivered on time—to stimulate your employees' competitive spirit.

b. Benchmark on-time delivery figures in your industry, then match your target to the average on-time delivery figure you've identified.

c. Set a range: 80 percent as the minimum target, 90 percent as the moderate target, and 99 percent as the "stretch" target.

8. You've collected data that reveals performance significantly below the target range you've set. How should you respond?

a. Investigate potential causes of the shortfall, including new processes, personnel changes, and technology shifts.

b. Decide that the target range was too aggressive overall and consider making it more moderate.

c. Identify a project or initiative that will enable your group to boost performance to meet or exceed the target range.

9. Which of the following approaches would you use to maintain your performance measurement method?

a. Keep your metrics consistent over time, so you can compare historical performance.

b. Modify objectives and performance metrics if necessary to reflect changing realities.

c. Change your metrics whenever you see an abrupt change in performance data.

10. Which of the following is an example of a leading performance indicator?

a. Customer-satisfaction ratings.

b. Revenues for the most recent quarter.

c. Number of new accounts established.

Answers to test questions

1, a. By measuring performance, companies determine the effectiveness of their strategies and operations and identify solutions to performance shortfalls and other problems. Organizations appraise their performance for numerous additional reasons—including determining whether to revise budgets and forecasts, identifying weak areas to gain a competitive edge over rivals, and distributing performance-based incentives and rewards fairly to employees.

2, b. A key performance indicator (KPI) is a representation of a critical success factor—the key determinant of success in achieving a strategic objective that a company or unit has defined. Organizations may have key performance indicators for all their areas of operation, or they may focus their KPIs on only one aspect of their operations. For example, a social service nonprofit might focus its KPIs on the amount of aid granted to different entities that it serves.

Many organizations use three types of KPIs: *Process* KPIs measure the efficiency or productivity of a business process (such as "Product-repair cycle time"). *Input* KPIs measure assets invested to generate business results (such as "Dollars spent on research and development"). *Output* KPIs measure the results of business activities (such as "Revenues").

3, c. Because a performance measurement (PM) system is applied throughout an entire organization, it enables executives to see how business results generated in the company's many different units combine to influence the enterprise's overall results. Thus a PM system gives executives and managers a comprehensive, high-level view of their organization's performance and an understanding of how the company's different parts work together to produce business results.

Commonly used PM systems include dashboards (also called cockpits) showing aggregated performance data; quality-improvement systems such as Six Sigma and the Baldrige National Quality Program; and the Balanced Scorecard.

4, b. In the first phase (deciding what to appraise), you define objectives for your group, define the actions to take to achieve those objectives, then define performance metrics to help you assess whether you're accomplishing those actions. In the second phase (gathering performance data), you set targets (desired performance) for each performance metric and collect performance data. In the third phase (interpreting performance data), you analyze the data you've collected to see how it compares with your targets, and you revise metrics and targets if needed to reflect new realities.

5, c. Performance metrics indicate how you'll determine whether you've carried out the critical activities needed to achieve your group's objectives. Metrics also indicate the kind of data you'll need to gather to evaluate performance. For example, the metric, "Number of employees who complete training with passing grade by end of quarter," could enable you to assess how well you're carrying out the critical activity, "Train employees on proper use of equipment," which could in turn support the objective "Reduce workplace accidents."

6, a. You can feel more confident about the validity of the data you're gathering if the data is up to date, available frequently enough for you to track performance on your metrics, and sufficiently detailed and accurate. Often, data provided by outside sources—

such as organizations that track companies' market share—can also be considered valid.

7, c. Setting a range of targets comprising a minimum, moderate, and "stretch" point can help your employees understand the varying levels of performance they must reach in order to achieve more ambitious goals. The "stretch" point in your target range can also help get your direct reports' competitive juices flowing: stretch targets represent a challenge and require considerable effort.

8, a. Gaps between actual and targeted performance indicate the need to investigate potential causes of the shortfall. For example, if your employees are making more mistakes than the targeted numbers, the problem may be stemming from confusion over how to use a new technology or piece of equipment. Or perhaps an unusual number of people were out on vacation during the evaluation period, and temps were brought in who weren't as familiar with the job. By identifying the causes of a performance shortfall, you can increase your chances of selecting the right intervention.

9, b. Business realities change—in the form of new technologies, shifting customer preferences, and new company or unit strategies. Your objectives and performance metrics should be relevant to current business conditions. However, you want to keep your objectives and metrics as consistent as possible over time so you can compare performance. Thus, you should strike a delicate balance: keep objectives and metrics consistent where possible and appropriate, but be willing to modify them if necessary to reflect changing realities.

10, a. Leading indicators suggest how your group's performance might change in the future. For example, the higher your customers' satisfaction, the greater the likelihood that they'll buy from your company again as well as spend more on their purchases, thus increasing profitability. Effective performance measurement systems contain a mix of leading indicators and lagging indicators. Lagging indicators look backward at what your company has achieved in the past—for example, revenues, number of new accounts established, sales, and so forth.

To Learn More

Articles

Campbell, Dennis. "Choose the Right Measures, Drive the Right Strategy." *Balanced Scorecard Report*, May–June 2006.

> Metrics overload is a common problem that can have serious consequences: specifically, it can make it difficult for employees to see what actions they should take to execute strategic objectives. Having too many metrics dilutes the focus and invariably means many are irrelevant. Here, accounting and performance measurement expert Dennis Campbell traces a major Canadian bank's experience in overhauling its customer satisfaction metrics to make them meaningful—and actionable—to front-line employees.

Carney, Karen. "Successful Performance Measurement: A Checklist." *Harvard Management Update*, November 1999.

> The ultimate purpose of your performance measurement system is to energize employees to excel. But to fulfill this purpose, your system must demonstrate certain characteristics. Carney provides a checklist for evaluating your system's effectiveness. Essential elements include targets and metrics that support big-picture goals that everyone understands

and objectives that are clear and reasonable. The article also provides guidelines for measuring "soft" aspects of performance—for example, using a scale of 1 to 5 to measure how well employees demonstrate key values such as accepting responsibility and pursuing growth aggressively.

Case, John. "Using Measurement to Boost Your Unit's Performance." *Harvard Management Update*, October 1998.

This article offers five tips for effective performance measurement: for example, create metrics that matter by ensuring that metrics are linked to your objectives, that they don't inadvertently drive negative behavior, and that they reflect leading as well as lagging indicators. Also set meaningful targets by analyzing past performance, competitors' performance, the performance of benchmark-level companies in similar businesses, your own capabilities and resources, and input from employees. And involve those closest to the front line in defining metrics and setting targets, while ensuring that metrics are tied to larger strategic objectives and that employees understand those objectives.

Dodd, Dominic, and Ken Favaro. "Managing the Right Tension." *Harvard Business Review*, December 2006.

Of all the competing objectives every company wants to achieve, three pairs stand out: profitability versus growth, the short term versus the long term, and the whole organization versus the units. In each case, progress on one front usually comes at the expense of progress on the other. The problem, the authors discovered, is not so much that managers don't recognize the tensions; those are all too familiar to anyone who has ever run a business. Rather, it is that managers frequently don't focus on the tension that matters most to their company. Even when they do identify the right tension, they usually make the mistake of prioritizing a "lead" objective within it, for example, profitability over growth. As a result, companies often end up moving first in this direction, then in that, and then back again, never quite resolving the tension. The authors describe how companies can select the right tension, what traps they may fall into when they focus on one side over the other, and how to escape these traps by managing to the bonds between objectives.

Kaplan, Robert S., and David P. Norton. "The Balanced Scorecard: Measures That Drive Performance." *Harvard Business Review* OnPoint Enhanced Edition. Boston: Harvard Business School Publishing, July 2005.

The authors shed light on the Balanced Scorecard—a performance measurement system that many companies use to manage execution of their strategy. Just as you can't fly an airplane with just one instrument gauge, you can't manage a company's, unit's, or group's performance with just one kind of metric. The Balanced Scorecard enables managers to create a set of interrelated metrics that provides a comprehensive view of how a company, unit, or group is performing. The scorecard methodology requires establishing objectives and metrics for four performance "perspectives": financial, customer, internal business processes, and workforce innovation and learning.

Stauffer, David. "Is Your Benchmarking Doing the Right Work?" *Harvard Management Update*, September 2003.

Though benchmarking can help you create performance metrics, set targets, and identify best practices, it can also lead you astray if you use it carelessly. Stauffer explains benchmarking's pitfalls and provides suggestions for avoiding them. For example, too many managers benchmark information that's easy to find, not the information that they need to establish an effective performance measurement system. Some managers also stop after obtaining statistics about performance: they don't dig for an underlying explanation of what makes "the best" better than the rest. Thus they can't replicate the practices that the benchmarked organization has applied to achieve its success. Stauffer also warns against expecting world-class enterprises to reveal how they've gotten to the top if you're not also willing to sharing your own best practices.

Books

Kaplan, Robert S., and David P. Norton. *The Strategy-Focused Organization: How Balanced Scorecard Companies Thrive in the New Business Environment*. Boston: Harvard Business School Press, 2001.

This book provides case studies and practices for using the Balanced Scorecard as a performance measurement system. The authors emphasize the importance of linking performance measurement to execution of corporate strategy through application of five key principles: (1) translate corporate strategy into operational terms, (2) align the entire organization to the strategy, (3) make strategy execution everyone's job, (4) make strategy execution a continual process, and (5) mobilize strategic change through strong, effective leadership.

Lynch, Richard L., and Kelvin F. Cross. *Measure Up! How to Measure Corporate Performance*, 2nd ed. Oxford: Blackwell Business, 1995.

Lynch and Cross have created a concise guide that is nevertheless packed with information on how to measure business performance. Chapters cover topics such as defining objectives, measuring the right aspects of performance, creating meaningful metrics, and tailoring other systems (such as rewards and accounting) to support your performance measurement approach.

Neely, Andy. *Business Performance Measurement: Theory and Practice*. Cambridge: Cambridge University Press, 2002.

The field of performance measurement has evolved rapidly in the last few years with the emergence of new methodologies and frameworks. This book provides a summary of the leading ideas in business performance measurement, theory, and practice. Experts from a range of fields—including accounting, operations management, marketing, strategy, and organizational behavior—provide their viewpoints. You'll find chapters describing and comparing a number of performance measurement systems, clarifying the practical applications of performance measurement, and explaining how to create a set of meaningful metrics. The book closes with several chapters examining emerging issues and trends in performance measurement.

Niven, Paul R. *Balanced Scorecard Step-by-Step: Maximizing Performance and Maintaining Results.* New York: John Wiley & Sons, 2002.

Niven provides insight on and practical solutions for developing performance objectives and metrics that faithfully translate your company's or unit's strategy, and for setting appropriate targets. Additional chapters offer advice for reporting performance data, using results to allocate resources, and linking rewards to performance.

Sources for Measuring Performance

The following sources aided in development of this book:

The Essentials of Finance and Budgeting. Business Literacy for HR Professionals Series. Boston: Harvard Business School Press and the Society for Human Resource Management, 2005.

"Focus Your Organization on Strategy—with the Balanced Scorecard," 3rd ed. *Harvard Business Review* OnPoint Collection. Boston: Harvard Business School Publishing, October 2005.

Gebelein, Susan H., et al. *Successful Manager's Handbook.* ePredix, 2004 edition. Minneapolis: Personnel Decisions International, 2004.

Kaplan, Robert S., and David P. Norton. *The Balanced Scorecard: Translating Strategy into Action.* Boston: Harvard Business School Press, 1996.

Lynch, Richard L., and Kelvin F. Cross. *Measure Up! How to Measure Corporate Performance,* 2nd ed. Oxford: Blackwell Business, 1995.

Neely, Andy. *Business Performance Measurement: Theory and Practice.* Cambridge: Cambridge University Press, 2002.

Niven, Paul R. *Balanced Scorecard Step-by-Step: Maximizing Performance and Maintaining Results.* New York: John Wiley & Sons, 2002.

http://www.isixsigma.com.

http://www.quality.nist.gov.

Key Terms

Balanced Scorecard. A performance measurement system that assumes that financial performance is just one part of the larger picture of organizational performance. The system seeks to balance a company's financial perspective with three additional perspectives: customer, internal processes, and workforce learning and development. See also *performance measurement system*.

Baldrige National Quality Program. A quality-improvement performance measurement system that defines criteria for high-quality business performance in areas such as leadership, strategic planning, customer focus, and knowledge management. The Malcolm Baldrige Award, along with its European equivalent, is a prestigious annual award that recognizes organizations for achievement in specific categories: manufacturing, small business, education, and health care. See also *performance measurement system*.

benchmarking. Using information from trade associations, industry publications, or the Internet, data from other groups in your company, and information from other sources to compare a group's, unit's, or company's performance data and metrics with those of other business entities. Many managers who use benchmarking do so in order to identify best practices that they want their group to emulate. Benchmarking is also helpful for creating performance metrics and setting targets. See also *performance metric* and *target*.

cockpit. See *dashboard*.

critical success factor (CSF). A key activity that a group, unit, or company must carry out to achieve its objectives. See also *objectives*.

dashboard. A performance measurement system that combines a company's metrics, targets, and performance data into one online or printed document, such as a spreadsheet, that is prepared on a regular basis. Also called cockpit. See also *performance measurement system*.

data validity. The quality of performance data. Valid data can be checked for its accuracy and reliability. For example, revenue data can be confirmed by tabulating invoices generated.

economic value added (EVA). An output KPI that expresses the value of a business activity that is left over after you subtract from it the cost of executing that activity and the cost of the physical and financial capital deployed to generate the profits. EVA can be expressed as net operating profit after taxes minus net operating assets multiplied by the weighted cost of capital. See also *output KPI*.

external data. Performance results generated outside a company, such as a third-party organization's rankings of companies' performance against competitors'. See also *internal data*.

financial performance. Business results related to a company's financial health, such as revenues, expenses, and profits. See also *nonfinancial performance*.

input KPI. A key performance indicator that measures the assets and resources a company has invested in or used to generate business results. Examples include dollars spent on research and development, funding for employee training, and quality of raw materials. See also *key performance indicator*.

internal data. Performance data generated within a company, such as sales, customer satisfaction, and number of new hires. See also *external data*.

key performance indicator (KPI). A measure reflecting how an organization is doing in a specific aspect of its performance. A KPI is expressed as a critical success factor—the key determinant of success in achieving any given strategic objective. See also *critical success factor, input KPI, output KPI,* and *process KPI*.

lagging indicator. A metric that looks "backward" in time at what a company has already achieved in the past, such as sales. See also *leading indicator*.

leading indicator. A metric that looks "forward" in time, suggesting the results a company may expect to see in the future. For example, customer-satisfaction ratings suggest how customers may buy from a company in the future. See also *lagging indicator*.

market share. The percentage of sales in a given industry segment or subsegment captured by your company. See also *output KPI*.

metric. See *performance metric*.

minimum target. The lowest point in a three-point target range that a group, unit, or company sets for a performance metric. See also *performance metric* and *target*.

moderate target. The midpoint in a three-point target range that a group, unit, or company sets for a performance metric. See also *performance metric* and *target*.

nonfinancial performance. Business results related to aspects of a company's health other than financial performance, such as employee knowledge, information systems, and customer relationships. See also *financial performance*.

objectives. Goals that a group, unit, or company wants to accomplish in order to improve performance. Objectives may be related to strategy, to customer service, to business processes, and so forth.

objective data. Performance data that is easy to quantify, such as revenues, expenses, and workforce head count.

output KPI. A key performance indicator that measures the financial and nonfinancial results of business activities. Examples include revenues, number of new customers acquired, and percentage increase in full-time employees. See also *key performance indicator*.

performance measurement system. A set of strategic objectives and performance metrics (including KPIs) applied throughout an entire enterprise.

performance metric. Indicators of a group's, unit's, or company's ability to carry out the critical activities needed to achieve its objectives. For example, the performance metric for the critical activity "Train employees on proper use of equipment" might be "Number of employees who complete training with passing grade."

Plan-Do-Check-Act. A quality-improvement performance measurement system comprising four steps: (1) Plan—Identify a performance problem and the processes affecting it; (2) Do—Explore potential solutions and implement one; (3) Check—Assess how well your solution worked; (4) Act—If your solution worked well, institutionalize it and look for another improvement opportunity. See also *performance measurement system*.

process KPI. A key performance indicator that measures the efficiency or productivity of a business process—for example, product-repair cycle time, days to deliver an order, or time to fill vacant positions. See also *key performance indicator*.

return on investment (ROI). An output KPI that represents the benefits generated from the use of assets in a company, unit, or group, or on a project. ROI is expressed as net income (revenues minus expenses and liabilities, such as taxes) divided by total assets. See also *output KPI*.

Six Sigma. A quality-improvement performance measurement system that stresses the continual improvement of business processes through reduction of errors. See also *performance measurement system*.

stretch target. The most ambitious point in a three-point target range set by a group, unit, or company for a performance metric. See also *performance metric* and *target*.

subjective data. Performance data that is difficult to quantify, such as customer satisfaction, employee morale, and product innovativeness. Leading indicators often require subjective data. See also *leading indicator* and *objective data*.

target. The performance that a group, unit, or company wants to achieve on a performance metric. Targets are often expressed as three-point ranges. For example, for the metric "Percentage of employees who complete training with passing grade," the target may be "80 percent minimum, 90 percent moderate, and 100 percent stretch." See also *minimum target, moderate target, performance metric,* and *stretch target.*

trend. Changes in performance data that form a pattern over time. For example, average error rate declines over six months. Managers examine trends to decide how to respond to gaps between target performance and actual performance.

Notes

Notes

Notes

Notes

Notes

Notes

Notes

How to Order

Harvard Business School Press publications are available world-wide from your local bookseller or online retailer.

You can also call:
1-800-668-6780

Our product consultants are available to help you 8:00 a.m.–6:00 p.m., Monday–Friday, Eastern Time. Outside the U.S. and Canada, call: 617-783-7450.

Please call about special discounts for quantities greater than ten.

You can order online at:
www.HBSPress.org